ANTIQUES AND THEIR VALUES

KITCHEN EQUIPMENT

COMPILED BY TONY CURTIS

While every care has been taken in compiling the information contained in this volume the publishers cannot accept any liability for loss, financial or otherwise, incurred by reliance placed on the information herein.

ISBN 0 902921 41 X

Copyright (C) Lyle Publications 1977

Published by Lyle Publications, Glenmayne, Galashiels, Selkirkshire, Scotland.

Printed by Apollo Press, Unit 5, Dominion Way, Worthing, Sussex.

INTRODUCTION

Congratulations! You now have in your hands an extremely valuable book. It is one of a series specially devised to aid the busy professional dealer in his everyday trading. It will also prove to be of great value to all collectors and those with goods to sell, for it is crammed with illustrations, brief descriptions and valuations of hundreds of antiques.

Every effort has been made to ensure that each specialised volume contains the widest possible variety of goods in its particular category though the greatest emphasis is placed on the middle bracket of trade goods rather than on those once - in - a - lifetime museum pieces whose values are of academic rather than practical interest to the vast majority of dealers and collectors.

This policy has been followed as a direct consequence of requests from dealers who sensibly realise that, no matter how comprehensive their knowledge, there is always a need for reliable, up-to-date reference works for identification and valuation purposes.

When using your Antiques and their Values to assess the worth of goods, please bear in mind that it would be impossible to place upon any item a precise value which would hold good under all circumstances. No antique has an exactly calculable value; its price is always the result of a compromise reached between buyer and seller, and questions of condition, local demand and the business acumen of the parties involved in a sale are all factors which affect the assessment of an object's 'worth' in terms of hard cash.

In the final analysis, however, such factors cancel out when large numbers of sales are taken into account by an experienced valuer, and it is possible to arrive at a surprisingly accurate assessment of current values of antiques; an assessment which may be taken confidently to be a fair indication of the worth of an object and which provides a reliable basis for negotiation.

Throughout this book, objects are grouped under category headings and, to expedite reference, they progress in price order within their own categories. Where the description states 'one of a pair' the value given is that for the pair sold as such.

CONTENTS

APPLE CORERS

Early 19th century apple corer, with ivory handle. £16

Silver and ivory corer, 1811. £44

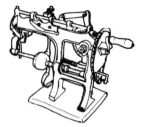

Apple corer made around 1890-1910 works on same principal as a sewing machine. £75

Silver apple corer, maker TH, circa 1710, 13.8cm. long. £95

Silver peeler and corer by Samuel Pemberton, 1803. £135

ASPARAGUS TONGS

Asparagus tongs by Mappin and Webb, Sheffield 1894. £48

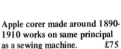

Silver asparagus tongs by G.W. Adams, 1864. £65

Silver asparagus servers by Thomas Northcote, 1790. £75

Silver asparagus tongs by William Chawner, 10½in. long, 5.5oz., 1832. £95

An oak and metal
bound wine cask
with tap, 1ft.8in.
£14

Victorian lead glazed
spirit barrel.   £18

Stoneware spirit
barrel, with a brass
tap, circa 1840.£24

Stoneware spirit barrel
with brass tap.   £35

One of a pair of
spirit barrels
moulded with the
Royal Arms and
Vines.   £38

A steel banded oak
cider barrel with
hand riveted joints
to bands, 11in.
diameter at top,
circa 1840.   £40

Late 19th century
cut glass barrel
with a gun metal
tap.   £40

Staffordshire white pottery
spirit barrel titled 'Brandy',
circa 1850, 12½in. high.£58

A Victorian vinegar
barrel, in sand-
coloured ironstone
with a raised Coat of
Arms.   £68

9

BASKETS

Victorian miniature basket, about 4in. across.   £1

Victorian clothes basket. £2

A Regency waste paper basket on scroll feet   £50

BELLOWS

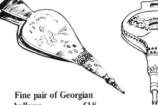

19th century elm bellows.   £16

Fine pair of Georgian bellows.   £18

Walnut bellows with carved landscape 'Auld Brig O'Doon'.   £20

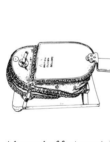

A large pair of foot operated bellows of elm and leather construction on baseboard, 1ft.9in. long, 1ft.2in. high.   £25

Elm bellows with centred brass decoration, 25 ins. long circa 1790.£35

19th century oak and brass mounted fire blower.   £35

Eastern brass bell and brass wall bracket. £9

Hand bell with turned wood handle, about 1840, 19cm. high. £10

A small, pierced and chased silver table bell. £18

Oriental bronze table bell, on carved and pierced ironwood stand. £28

Large bronze muffin man's hand bell by Mears and Son. £35

George II silver table bell by Thomas Whipham, 5½ oz. £560

BOOT ACCESSORIES

Victorian cast iron boot scraper. £12

19th century mahogany bootrack. £45

One of a pair of George IV boot jacks by Paul Storr, 7½in. long, London 1825. £200

BLUE & WHITE CHINA

Spode, blue and white egg stand. £8.50

Staffordshire soup bowl, circa 1825. £3

One of a pair of Ringtons square-shaped tea caddies transferred in blue, 10cm. high. £9

Blue and white transfer printed small oval dish, impressed Copeland, and number 6, circa 1850, 8½in. long. £12

One of a pair of late 19th century blue and white Delft style candlesticks. £15

Blue and white pictorial Spode ware ashet. £15

A marked Wedgwood ashet, 8in. long. £15

Small fan-shaped asparagus server in Caughley porcelain, circa 1780-90. £20

Stone china turkey dish by Knight, Elkin and Co., circa 1830. £23

Caughley porcelain egg-drainer and 'waster', circa 1780-90. £25

A 19th century Worcester blue and white pickle dish. £40

"Tower" two-handled covered centre bowl, marked Spode. £45

A marked Spode comport, 'Long Elizas'. £45

A very rare marked Spode "Forest Landscape" dog's dish. £55

English Delftware, four division sweetmeat dish on three feet, Liverpool, about 1750-60. £130

Rare Chelsea blue and white bowl of octagonal form with galleried rim, circa 1750, 4¾in. high. £540

Lowestoft blue and white mug, circa 1765-68. £560

Lowestoft blue and white coffee pot, circa 1757-60. £1,350

BOTTLES

Early light amber glass 'Bovril' jar.£1

Brown glass beer bottle.£1

Small green tinted glass sauce bottle. £0.75

Small mineral water bottle.£1

Sheared top sauce bottle of green tinted glass.   £1

Victorian whisky bottle.   £4

'Dumpy' green glass mineral water bottle.   £4

Green glass 'onion' bottle, circa 1885.£4

Dark green glass pickle jar 1880.£6

Codd's glass mineral bottle with amber stopper. £12

Victorian embossed black glass whisky bottle. £15

Sealed bottle marked with letter 'S', about 1800, 10½in. high. £25

Codd's amber glass mineral bottle. £30

Prices Patent Candle Co. cough medicine bottle in cobalt blue. £30

Wine bottle by Henry Ricketts of Bristol, 1811, 9in. high. £38

Handblown bottle, about 1810, with ribboning decoration, 12in. high. £85

Bottle with 'John Cumm, 1770' engraved on it, 9in. high. £150

Sealed bottle dated 1828 and initialled A. Cumm, 9½in. high. £200

BOWLS

Victorian earthenware mixing bowl. £2.50

'Quick-cooker' for making steak and kidney pudding, around 1890. £3.50

A Devonmoor pottery earthenware bowl, with applied and incised decoration. £10

Wooden dairy bowl. £11

An unusually large Welsh butter bowl of sycamore wood, circa 1790, 17in. diameter. £28

A Sunderland ware bowl, with transfer printed panels, 12½in. diameter. £40

Brass and copper bowl on lion paw feet, 18in. diam. £45

Ruskin eggshell pottery bowl, circa 1910. £50

Liverpool bowl by William Ball, circa 1760. £420

BREAD BINS

BREAD BINS

Early 20th century enamel bread bin £5

Victorian 'Improved Bread Pan' in earthenware. £9

A heavily chased and embossed plated bread bin and cover. £48

BREAD HUTCHES

French 18th century bread hutch in walnut, 32in. wide. £450

Early oak food hutch. £650

BREAD PEELS

Oven peel used in a brick oven. £20

A large wooden bread peel. £24

17

BUCKETS

Victorian Fireman's leather bucket decorated with a Coat of Arms.   £35

An old tin and wrought iron well bucket, 18in. high.   £45

A fine polished sheet iron well bucket, with wrought iron swing handle and hook, circa 1780, 16in. high excluding handle. £50

An attractive well bucket, with wrought iron swing handle and decorative riveted strength bands, circa 1790, 17in. high. £60

Dutch circular copper bucket with swing handle, 15in. diam.£70

Dutch copper and brass peat bucket, circa 1770, 16in. high.   £90

A fine 18th century brass bucket. £175

18th century mahogany brass bound bucket.   £195

George III mahogany bucket with brass fittings, circa 1790.   £325

Late 18th century
brass bound maho-
gany plate bucket.
£180

Butler's brass bound
mahogany plate
bucket with a
tapered handle and
original brasses,
circa 1745.   £195

A brass handled
and banded
mahogany plate
pail, circa 1755.
£200

BUTTERCHURNS

Butter worker used
on a sloping tray. £5

Table type box churn,
late 19th century. £8

Glass butter churn
mounted on an
iron stand.   £18

Early Victorian Scottish
butter churn in pine,
48cm. high x 34cm.
wide x 43cm. deep. £40

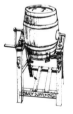

Late 19th century
Champion butter
churn.   £45

19th century sand-
blasted butter
churn.   £80

BUTTER DISHES

Victorian brown
earthenware
butter dish. £2

Blue and white china butter
dish, circa 1890.   £3

Victorian butter
dish with cow,
no mark. £10

Glass butter dish,
cover and stand,
circa 1810. £38

Brass banded oak
butter dish, circa
1840.   £48

Silver revolving
butter tureen,
by Atkin Bros.,
Sheffield, 1893.
                £550

BUTTER PATS

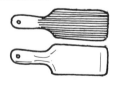

Butter pats for shaping.   £2   Pair of Victorian butter pats. £2.50

Victorian glove button hook with pearl handle.   £7

Silver Art Nouveau button hook with Birmingham made handle.
£12

CAKE STANDS

A mahogany circular, three tier cakestand.
£15

Edwardian inlaid three tier cake stand.   £22

19th century brass three tier cake stand.   £28

CANDELABRUM

Ormolu candelabrum for two lights on a marble base, 14½in. high.   £7

A French ormolu candelabrum for three lights, on triangular shaped base, 19¾in. high.   £70

An important pair of 19th century brass candelabra, 1ft.8in. high.   £150

CANDLE BOXES

Japanned candle box in black and red. £6

19th century brass candle holder. £15

18th century elm taper box. £30

CANDLE EXTINGUISHERS

Unnamed pottery candle extinguisher. £1

Candle extinguisher by Davenport with cone-shaped stand. £10

Candle extinguisher with naturally coloured face, 1885. £160

CANDLE STANDS

Single brass adjustable candlestick stand, the shaped lobed base covering iron weight, circa 1820, 9in. high. £30

Georgian mahogany candle stand. £38

William and Mary candle stand in walnut with quarter veneered top and inlaid herringbone. £375

Pair of oak candlesticks with barleysugar twist stems and brass drip pans.   £5.50

Pair of moulded brass table candlesticks on scroll feet, 11in. high.   £12

A pair of 19th century brass table candlesticks on circular bases, 6½in. high.   £14

A pair of brass candlesticks with open spiral stems, 12in. high.   £16

A pair of 19th century brass candlesticks on circular bases, 9½in. high.   £19

A pair of brass candlesticks on circular bases, 10¾in. high. £22

A single Queen Anne side pusher brass candlestick on an octagonal base, circa 1720, 6¾in. high.   £28

A pair of 19th century brass candlesticks on octagonal bases, 12½in. high.   £35

George I single brass candlestick, steeped cast brass, smooth underneath, circa 1725, 7in. high. £35

CANDLESTICKS

Pair of embossed bronze candlesticks entwined with dragons. £38

A fine pair of Adam style brass candlesticks, the fluted stem connecting to the stepped base with beading decoration, circa 1770, 10½in. high. £50

Pair of tall George II bell metal candlesticks with turned inside circular bases, 9¾in. high. £55

Pair of early 19th century French ormolu candlesticks with detachable sconces, circa 1810, 11¾in. high. £55

An unusual pair of wine cellarman's candlesticks with steel stems to the top, with brass sconces and drip pans, circa 1810, 9½in. high. £55

Large pair of cylindrical brass candlesticks, circa 1870. £60

Pair of early Victorian brass candlesticks to take glass storm shades, 10½in. high. £60

A brass candlestick with four ejection holes in the sconce, circa 1685, 7½in. high. £75

Pair of Georgian brass candlesticks with petal shaped bases, circa 1740. £100

A fine pair of drip pan candlesticks, with cast brass baluster stems and turned cast domed bases, 9in. high.   £105

A pair of French ormolu candlesticks with figures of children, on a shaped base, 8in. high.   £105

A pair of brass candlesticks, circa 1740.   £110

A large pair of 17th century brass drip pan candlesticks, mounted on four claw feet, 6in. diameter.   £135

Pair of 17th century brass candlesticks with barley-sugar twist stems and embossed cast brass bases, 10in. high.   £140

A pair of George I brass candlesticks with knopped stems.   £190

Pair of Persian brass candlesticks with hand-engraved Arabic inscriptions, 14½in. high, circa 1680.   £265

A Flemish brass candlestick, circa 1500, 21cm. high.   £440

Pair of bronze pricket candlesticks, 15th century.   £900

25

CARDBOARD BOXES

Lever Brothers 'Lux' soap flakes, circa 1910. £2

Lever Brothers 'Sunlight Soap', circa 1890. £2

Lever Brothers 'Lifebuoy Soap', circa 1910. £2

Lever Brothers 'Plantol' soap, circa 1900. £3

CARVING SETS

19th century plated bread knife, fork and cheese scoop with ivory handles. £13

Victorian carving set with bone handles. £15

Victorian carving knife and fork with chased handles. £19

Early 18th century knife and fork, probably German, circa 1710. £110

CAULDRONS

CAULDRONS

A 16th century cast iron cooking cauldron, with original hand wrought swing handle, standing on three feet, 13in. high, 9¼in. diameter.   £65

16th century polished cast iron cauldron, with swing handle, 11in. diameter.   £70

George III copper cauldron and lid, circa 1770, 22in. wide.   £95

CHARGERS

18th century pewter charger with deep central bowl, 13in. diameter.   £24

A large Imari charger.   £150

English Delft charger with figure of William III, 13¾in. high.   £336

CHAMBER POTS

Victorian chamber pot.   £5

Decorative Victorian china chamber pot. £8

A blue and white transfer printed chamber pot, unmarked.   £40

CHAMBERSTICKS

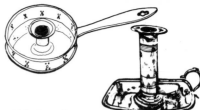

Late Victorian
green enamel
chamberstick. £3

19th century brass
chamber candlestick
with handle.   £7

Brass chamber stick
with a drip pan. £10

A 19th century
copper chamber
candlestick. £11

Victorian brass
chamber candle
lamp with cone
snuffer.   £16

Victorian plated
chamberstick and
snuffer.   £18

Sheffield plate
chamberstick,
circa 1810. £39

Mid 18th century
copper chamberstick
with pierced decor-
ation, 7½in. long.
     £135

Silver chamberstick
by Emes and Barnard,
London 1822.   £270

Victorian floral
china cheese cover.
£4

Blue and white china
cheese dish and cover,
circa 1890.   £6

Crown Devon
pottery cheese
cover.   £7

Marked Spode cheese
dish base, 'Driving A
Bear From Sugar
Canes'.   £28

Large Victorian
cheese dish. £35

Large Victorian
earthenware cheese
dish and cover
with green and
brown decoration.
£40

An unusual pottery cheese
dish and cover, with white
orange skin body and polychrome raised Japanese
stylised flowers, 9in. high.
£40

Large late 18th
century blue and
white cheese dish.
£50

19th century Jasper
ware Stilton dish from
the Minton factory,
12in. long, 12in. high.
£85

CHEESE PRESSES

Mid 19th century
polished steel
press.   £35

An interesting farmhouse
cheese press, with wrought
iron frame, 20in. high,
circa 1800.   £48

18th century hand
wrought steel cheese
press complete with
large brass bowl,
56in. high, circa 1720.
                    £250

CHEESE SCOOPS

Small long-handled silver scoop,
Birmingham, 1904.   £10

Victorian silver cheese scoop with
ivory handle.   £30

Stilton cheese scoop with ejector
slide, Joseph Taylor, Birmingham
1803.   £52

Irish silver cheese scoop,
John Dalrymple, Dublin
1793.   £62

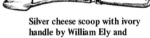

Silver cheese scoop with ivory
handle by William Ely and
William Fearn, 1804, 10¼in.
long.   £80

Silver cheese scoop with ivory
handle by TF, 1808.   £90

CHESTNUT ROASTERS

Victorian polished steel chestnut
roaster.   £8

Brass circular chestnut roaster with
iron handle.   £15

30

19th century Wedgwood majolica fish dish. £4

Stoneware ale barrel tap impressed "Doulton & Co., Lambeth, London", circa 1869. £20

Minton sardine dish and cover decorated in polychrome, 23.5cm. wide. £24

Blue and white porcelain potato ring, Ch'ien Lung, 8½in. diameter. £24

A Cunerville sauceboat with two jugs. £24

A white and gilt Copeland spoon warmer in the form of a large sea shell, on sea-weed and coral base, circa 1850, 4½in. high. £35

Late 18th century slipware baking dish with a trellis design, 14½in. wide. £200

Rare saltglaze porringer of small size in white, circa 1745, 4in. wide. £300

Lowestoft Pap warmer, 10¼in. high, circa 1765. £400

CHOCOLATE MOULDS

An unusual chocolate mould, possibly German, in the shape of a lion.   £10

A pelican-shaped chocolate mould, possibly German.   £10

An unusual chocolate mould in the shape of a dog, possibly of German manufacture.   £10

CLEAVERS

Small, Victorian butcher's cleaver.   £4.50

Victorian, cast iron, butcher's cleaver.   £4.50

A small 19th century, butcher's chopper in steel with turned oak handle, 13in. long.   £15

19th century, butcher's cleaver.   £17

19th century, butcher's cleaver.   £18

Exceptionally large, old, butcher's cleaver, 26in. high.   £18

Victorian circular wall
clock by Jump, London.
£20

Victorian rosewood
octagonal wall
clock.   £30

A walnut inlaid
wall clock with
enamelled dial.
£40

Regency mahogany
and brass inlaid wall
clock with circular
dial, 1ft.11in. high.
£45

A Victorian walnut
and floral marquetry
wall clock with
enamel dial, 75cm.
high.   £50

Wall clock with circular
yew frame, painted dial
with black Roman
numerals.   £55

A Victorian walnut
cased wall clock with
fluted pillars, enamel
dial and brass pendu-
lum.   £70

Mahogany wall
clock with convex
dial and glass. £115

Well-figured walnut striking
Vienna regulator.   £185

33

COAL BOXES AND CABINETS

Late Victorian oak coal box with brass fittings.   £18

A late 19th century brass tapered coal box and cover, standing on paw feet.   £18

Edwardian walnut coal cabinet with brass back-rail, handles and shovel.   £18

Victorian walnut coal depot with brass handle and coal scoop.   £20

Victorian brass coal vase and cover with handles, on three paw feet.   £20

Victorian, black japanned coal box.   £22

Victorian, brass circular double-handled box and cover with handles. £22

Edwardian rosewood coal cabinet inlaid with boxwood.   £24

Late Victorian painted coal box complete with shovel.   £25

Victorian circular brass coal box and cover.£32

Art Nouveau design copper circular coal vase, 56cm. high.£32

Victorian japanned coal depot with china handle.   £40

Ornate Regency brass coal box with shovel and embossed flap.   £45

Late Victorian cast iron coal box.   £45

19th century oval polished steel coal box, 14in. high.   £70

19th century mahogany serpentine fronted coal cabinet with an ormolu gallery and mounts, 1ft. 4in. wide.   £70

A Pontypool coal bin.   £80

French ormolu coal box, 24in. high.   £100

COAL PAILS

Victorian Barge ware coal pail. £20

19th century copper pail with swing handle. £20

19th century copper coal pail with a brass handle. £20

A fine copper coal hod with brass loop handles, 1ft.9in. high. £22

19th century stained wood and brass bound coal pail with brass handle. £22

Circular copper coal pail. £27

Copper and brass bound oval coal pail with swing handle. £30

Late 18th century copper coal hod. £34

A 19th century embossed brass, oval coal pail, with double hinged covers and handle. £55

A 19th century brass coal helmet with swing handle.   £15

Victorian copper scoop coal scuttle with a swing handle.   £20

A copper coal helmet with swing handle.   £30

Early 19th century brass coal helmet.   £30

19th century brass coal helmet with a swing handle. £32

Copper helmet shaped coal scuttle, circa 1810.   £35

George III copper coal scuttle.   £35

George III brass coal scuttle. £35

Large Victorian brass coal scuttle.   £38

37

COAL SCUTTLES

Early 19th century
copper coal helmet.
£38

18th century helmet
coal scuttle with
ebony handle. £45

Copper coal scuttle,
circa 1800.   £45

Early 19th century
copper helmet coal
scuttle.   £45

A Victorian brass
coal helmet, with
swing handle. £45

Late 18th century
copper coal
helmet.   £48

Attractive angular
shaped copper coal
scuttle, circa 1820,
21in. long, 19in.
high.   £50

A fine Georgian
copper coal scuttle
with brass handle grips,
19in. long, 17in. high.
£60

18th century oval
copper scuttle of
rare and unusual
design.   £80

38

COFFEE GRINDERS

COFFEE GRINDERS

Mid Victorian
coffee grinder.
£20

Cast iron and brass
coffee grinder, 5in.
square.   £35

A rare, polished
iron coffee bean
roaster, circa
1760.   £60

A large 19th century
iron and brass tub
wheel coffee mill.£60

A fine Victorian
brass and steel
coffee grinder,
26in. high. £75

Coffee merchant's
grinder with ori-
ginal paintwork,
27in. high. £125

COFFEE POTS

An Indian copper
and plated vase-
shaped coffee
pot.   £16

George III tavern
coffee pot in
copper, 10in.
high.   £70

Large copper
Scandinavian coffee
kettle, about 1770,
14in. high.   £100

CORKSCREWS

Victorian steel corkscrew. £1.50

Late 19th century plated pocket corkscrew. £3

Victorian corkscrew with horn handle and brush, about 1860. £10

19th century staghorn corkscrew. £11

Thomason's Patent continuous double action corkscrew with ivory handle and brush. £32

Victorian double action brass corkscrew. £36

Huntsman's cut steel pocket tool kit with eight folding tools, circa 1820. £47

Charles Hull, 1864 patent, single lever corkscrew. £205

Mid 19th century French bronze corkscrew. £1,050

CRUMB SCOOPS

CRUMB SCOOPS

Victorian brass crumb scoop. £2.50

Victorian brass crumb scoop. £5

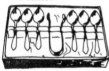

Art Nouveau brass crumb scoop.
£7.50

Victorian silver crumb scoop with
ivory handle. £18

CUTLERY

Cased set of six
silver coffee
spoons and sugar
tongs with fluted
handles. £11

Cased set of twelve
fish knives and forks
with ivory handles. £18

Cased set of
Victorian silver
servers. £18

Cased set of twelve
silver coffee spoons.
£22

Twelve plated dessert
knives and twelve
forks in oak case. £26

George III silver
christening set.
£30

Staffordshire willow pattern cup and saucer, circa 1860. £3

Illustrated cup and saucer by Adam Buck, 1830. £3.50

Famille rose coffee cup and saucer decorated with flowers. £8

Early 19th century porcelain cup and saucer, painted with flowers. £9

Lowestoft tea bowl and saucer decorated in the Chinese style. £32

1st period Worcester coffee cup and saucer painted in a Kakiemon palette. £90

Early 19th century Pinxton cup and saucer painted with a landscape medallion. £95

19th century Berlin cup and saucer. £125

Longton Hall tea bowl and saucer, circa 1750. £170

DISPENSERS

DISPENSERS

2½ gallon iron fountain. £18

Large copper and brass hot punch dispenser, complete with burner, 20in. high, circa 1840. £85

Late 18th century water cistern with tap, 9in. high. £150

DOOR FURNITURE

Pair of 18th century brass door handles. £5

Art Nouveau bronze door handle, 35cm. long. £9.50

Victorian cast iron door knocker, circa 1850, 8in. high. £12

Finely detailed Adam period door knocker, 9in. high. £27

George III brass door lock, 7in. wide, with keeper and key. £38

French steel-cased door lock with heavy ormolu trim, brass handles, and escutcheon plate, circa 1790. £58

DOOR STOPS

A solid cast brass standing plaque, stamped on back 'Crowley & Co., Manchester', circa 1860, 9in. long, 7in. high. £13

Victorian cast iron door stop, 9in. high. £14

Victorian brass dog door poster. £14

19th century cast iron door stop depicting a rampant lion. £17

Victorian cast iron door stop of a horse, on a stepped base, 11¼in. long, 10in. high. £20

A 19th century brass dolphin door stopper. £30

A good cast iron figure of a horse, standing on a modelled base, 1ft. 8in. long. £32

A historical cast brass door stop of King George IV leaning on a pillar, 7½in. long, 8in. high. £32

One of a pair of heavy cast iron door stops of zebras, circa 1820, 10½in. long, 8in. high. £50

44

A sugar bowl from the Dartmouth pottery, bearing the legend, 'Waste not, want not.'   £2

Saltglazed 7lb. jar.   £2

Victorian stoneware hot water bottle.£4

An unmarked pottery hot water jug. £5

An unmarked earthenware coffee pot, the motto cut through the white slip to the brown clay.   £6

Stoneware pot for bone marrow, 10in. high.   £7

Large Victorian earthenware storage jar.   £10

Victorian earthenware game dish.   £35

Liverpool earthenware lead glaze jug, circa 1700.   £60

Victorian pierced brass fender. £30

Late 19th century wrought iron half circle fender, 2ft.4in. wide. £12

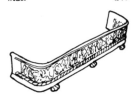

Victorian brass fender, 4ft.6in. wide. £40

Victorian cast iron fender. £40

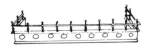

19th century brass fender with pierced foliage design. £42

Victorian brass fender with rail, 177cm. wide. £60

19th century brass club fender with a leather upholstered top. £120

English, shaped front brass club fender, with lion mask and green leather studded seats, circa 1865. £225

Pair of 18th century
andirons.   £20

Victorian iron and
brass firedogs. £8

A pair of cast iron fire rests
with winged lion head fronts
and brass mounts.   £20

Wrought iron andirons,
circa 1710, 16in. high.
£38

An exceptionally fine pair
of hand wrought firedogs
of Elizabeth I period, with
spit hooks, 29in. high,
circa 1570.   £225

A pair of polished steel
firedogs of the Art
Nouveau period, design
by Ernest Gimson and
made by Alfred Bucknell,
circa 1910.   £700

FIRE IRONS

A set of three fire
implements with
Adam style handles.
£30

Early 19th century
brass fire irons com-
plete with matching
stand.   £40

A fine set of polished
steel fire irons on a
stand, circa 1840. £50

FIRE GRATES

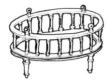

An iron basket grate, 2ft. wide. £38

Early 19th century brass and iron grate. £95

George III brass and iron grate. £110

Regency period brass basket grate, 1ft.10in. wide. £150

Regency style 'X' frame grate. £155

Late 18th century Adam design day grate. £210

Adam style brass day grate. £250

An attractive polished steel fire grate, standing on two Adam style tapering fluted legs, with urns surmounting each one, circa 1790. £275

George III serpentine-fronted basket grate, with brass facing, circa 1780, 32in. high, 28in. wide. £300

20th century firescreen with tapestry decoration. £9

Late 19th century pressed brass firescreen. £12

19th century mahogany cheval firescreen with crimson cloth panels.£14

19th century brass fireguard, 3ft.6in. wide. £18

Victorian mirror firescreen hand-painted with roses. £18

Two-fold bamboo firescreen with painted glass panels. £25

Victorian brass two-fold firescreen. £35

A mahogany framed fire-screen containing a glazed trumpet banner of the Household Cavalry, 38 x 26in. £125

Empire style pierced brass firescreen, 16½in. high. £550

49

A black and red veined mantelpiece, with cast iron fireplace. £40

A white painted wood mantelpiece applied with mounts in relief, of Adam design with urns, 42in. high, 56in. wide. £75

19th century cast iron fireplace with maroon tiles and brass ornamentation. £100

A 19th century carved pine Gothic style chimney piece, 4ft.3in. high, 5ft.8in. wide. £100

19th century carved oak fire surround. £185

Late 18th century French carved walnut fire surround, 40in. high. £200

A 19th century Adam style cast iron chimney piece painted to simulate marble, 4ft.5in, high, 5ft.4in. wide.   £200

A good quality late Regency period statuary marble chimney piece with original register grate en suite, 4ft. high, 5ft.8in. wide.   £230

Mason's ironstone fireplace surround, the side pillars in blue, with coloured flowers in relief and surmounted by a grotesque mask, 65in. wide.   £525

An Adam period statuary marble and jasper chimney piece with original register grate en suite, 4ft.11in. high, 5ft.10in. wide.   £1,250

Neo classical carved pine chimney piece, about 1785.   £2,200

Pietro Bossi's chimney piece with brass and iron grate.   £4,725

FIRES

Late 19th century cast iron stove with steel fittings. £30

Hastener in sheet iron with a brass bottle-jack above, 1880, 370cm. high x 155cm. wide x 99cm. deep. £105

An unusual French Empire peat burning fire. £150

FISH PANS

Victorian copper chafing dish, 13in. wide. £20

A large oval copper salmon pan with brass loop handles. £25

An early copper fish kettle and lid with bell metal carrying handles, 20in. wide. £55

FLASKS

Pressed glass flask, 7½in. high, cork insert for stopper, about 1896. £6

Stoneware spirit flask moulded on each side to show Rice, an American entertainer, 8in. high. £50

Stoneware spirit flask, depicting Daniel O'Connell. £85

A steel kettle stand, with brass handles and cabriole legs. £20

A small George II steel footman, 13½in. x 10½in. £25

George II steel footman with five 1in. flat slats across the top, standing on cabriole front legs, circa 1740, 18½in. wide, 12in. deep, 13½in. high. £35

Unusual copper, steel and brass cabriole leg footman with a single drawer. £50

19th century polished brass footman. £55

19th century footman with griddle. £65

Cast and wrought iron footman, circa 1820, 12in. long. £68

Late 18th century brass tavern footman. £75

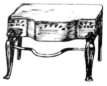

Pierced brass George III footman with handles. £75

53

FORKS

Victorian bread fork with wooden handle. £3

Silver pickle fork with ivory handle, about 1820. £6

Silver butter fork, Sheffield, 1865. £7

Silver salmon fork with bone handle, late Victorian. £7.50

A polished steel steak fork with turned screw type handle, circa 1840, 24in. long. £10

Pair of George IV pickle forks, 4½in. long, Dublin 1824, by M. West. £25

18th century meat fork. £32

Four prong 28in. long steel steak fork, circa 1710. £34

17th century steel steak fork, ram's horn top, circa 1660. £35

Pair of 18th century oyster forks, Old English thread. £35

A very rare Queen Anne period hand wrought eel spear, 23in. long. £50

17th century silver sucket fork with rat tail bowl, by T A., London 1690. £230

Victorian copper
frying pan with
iron handle. £14

An early copper
frying pan with
iron handle. £16

Copper frying pan,
circa 1780.   £38

GLASS UTENSILS

Glass toddy
stick. £0.25

Pair of cut glass pickle
jars and covers on a
plated stand.   £10

A cranberry coloured
murano type jam dish
in an EPNS holder
with spoon.   £15

Victorian glass fly
catcher.   £20

Pair of apothecary jars
marked 'Castor Oil
Seeds' and 'Cassia', with
original contents, 10in.
high.   £195

Coffee and cream
glass centrepiece
by Webbs, 10¼in.
diameter.   £260

55

GONGS

A Victorian brass table gong on an oak base.   £18

Bronze table gong supported by two carved elephants, 2ft.11in. wide. £28

Victorian brass gong complete with striker.   £38

Burmese brass gong supported by carved ivory tusks.   £45

GOBLETS

A 19th century yew wood goblet.   £7

A walnut goblet on stem.   £10

A Scottish carved wood goblet on a stem, 10¼in. high.   £20

GRAPE HODS

19th century oak and copper grape hod. £50

A copper grape hod, 35in. high. £55

GRAPE HODS

An embossed brass grape carrier. £65

GRIDDLES

19th century iron griddle. £15

19th century steel griddle iron. £23

18th century iron steak griddle, circa 1720. £37

HEATERS

Late 19th century brass framed heater on paw feet. £30

Victorian 'Ardent' brass heating lamp on a wrought iron stand with a copper top. £40

Victorian cast iron Cathedral heater. £55

HONEY POTS

Belleek honey pot,
5in. high.   £20

Silver plated honey
pot with green glass
body.   £65

An iridescent glass
honey pot.   £130

HOOKS

Queen Anne period
steel game hook.£15

A saw-type pot hanger
of polished steel, circa
1690, 26in. long.   £25

Fine fisherman's
salmon gaff, 16½in.
long, circa 1840. £35

ICE CREAM EQUIPMENT

Late 19th century
ice cream scoop.
                    £2

Late 19th century
ice cream mould
of tin.   £4

Late 19th century
ice cream maker.
                   £20

IRON STANDS

Green enamelled iron stand with pierced design. £4

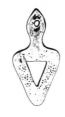

19th century sheet steel flat iron stand with triangular pierced motif, 8½in. long. £5

IRON STANDS

19th century cast brass flat iron stand with pierced star motif and heavy peg legs, 9¾in. long. £9

IRONS

Victorian flat iron. £3

Small Victorian smoothing iron. £4

William Cross & Sons 'Hot Cross' gas iron. £6

A large 18lb. goose iron. £8

Victorian box iron. £12

19th century iron complete with heating stone and stand. £14

IRONS

A box iron by Kenrick, size 6, circa 1870. £14

An early Scottish box iron. £14

Petrol heated iron, by Coleman, model 8 'Instant Lite'. £15

An early Dutch box iron. £16

Georgian brass goffering iron, circa 1830. £20

An early iron and brass flat iron. £20

A fine early iron and brass flat iron. £25

American fluting iron, circa 1870. £30

An unusual brass iron of about 1720 with original stone. £45

Royal Doulton art pot about 1902-22, 7½in. high x 8½in. deep.   £12

Victorian hanging art pot by the Watcombe Pottery Co., about 1867-1901, 7in. high x 9in. deep. £22

Minton art pot, dating between 1895-1900, in a single shade of mint green, 8½in. high. £23

A Maling lustre jardiniere decorated with fruits and foliage, 22.5cm. diam.   £24

Doulton (Lambeth) art pot, about 1880-91, 8½in. high x 10in. deep.   £35

Late 19th century jardiniere, 14½in. high x 17in. deep.   £45

Belleek porcelain jardiniere with birds and flowers in high relief, 20in. high.   £48

Attractive Art Nouveau Minton jardiniere, about 1900-08, 12½in. high x 14½in. deep. £75

Chinese blue and white jardiniere, 1830.   £100

JARDINIERES

COPPER AND BRASS

19th century Indian brass jardiniere with mask handles.   £12

19th century Benares ware brass jardiniere.   £14

A 19th century embossed copper circular jardiniere, 13in.   £14

Stylish brass jardiniere about 1900, with three supports and pierced-work band round the body.   £18

Victorian embossed brass jardiniere on paw feet, 12in. wide.   £18

Indian brass circular jardiniere with animal masks and ring handles, 36cm. diameter.   £18

Copper circular jardiniere with brass lions' masks and paw feet, 32cm. high.   £30

Copper jardiniere of about 1800, 16in. high.   £75

Regency brass and copper jardiniere with embossed Coat of Arms, 10in. high.   £80

Victorian china
jelly mould. £4

Edwardian glass rabbit
jelly mould.   £5

Victorian copper
jelly mould.   £14

19th century copper
jelly mould.   £21

Victorian copper
jelly mould.   £16

Large Victorian
copper jelly mould.
                    £17

19th century copper
jelly mould.   £21

Victorian copper
jelly mould. £22

Large Victorian
copper jelly mould.
                  £26

Copeland pineapple
jelly mould, circa
1860.   £28

Victorian milk jug
with a pewter lid.
£7

Victorian basin jug
decorated with hand
painted floral designs.
£8.50

19th century stone-
ware quart jug. £18

Caughley cream jug in
underglaze blue, circa
1780, 3¼in. high. £26

Liverpool earthenware
lead glaze jug, circa
1700.   £60

Liverpool creamware
jug, transfer printed
in black, circa 1785.
£85

Bristol jug decorated
with swags of flowers
in polychrome, 4¾in.
high.   £105

A Coalport jug
printed in dark
blue, 21.5cm.
high. £110

Martin Brothers
mask jug, 6¼in.
high. £385

An Art Nouveau
copper water jug,
12in. high.   £10

An Eastern copper and
brass jug with domed
cover.   £12

A copper, Jersey
pattern milk jug,
10in. high.   £12

A 19th century
copper jug with
loop handle and
rivetted band,
11in. high.   £18

18th century copper
hot water jug.   £19

A very unusual shaped,
copper spirit jug with
tinned interior, circa
1840, 8in. high.   £25

19th century brass
jug with tapered
body and dome,
hinged cover.   £30

Fine copper wine flagon,
brass handle, base and
rim, 12½in. high, circa
1710.   £80

Swiss cylindrical
bell jug,
circa 1735.£140

KETTLES

Early 20th century
red enamel kettle
with folding handle
£5

Late 19th century
brass kettle.   £9

Small Victorian
copper kettle.£22

A fine Victorian brass
kettle and stand.   £25

Brass circular
kettle with amber
handle.   £25

19th century iron
hob kettle and
pot hook.   £30

Cook's cast iron
hot water kettle,
of two gallon
capacity, with
wrought iron swing
handle.   £35

Heavy 19th century
brass spirit kettle
supported by two
monkeys, on a
stand complete with
burner.   £35

A copper kettle,
the lid with
pineapple finial.
£35

A fine quality copper kettle with a brass spout. £40

Unusually large early 19th century square copper kettle. £40

Georgian copper kettle with acorn lid. £40

Very fine three gallon hot water kettle made of cast iron, 18in. high, circa 1840. £40

Large George III copper kettle with fishtail spout. £44

19th century copper and brass kettle with matching stand and burner. £45

Brass spirit kettle, with glass handle, circa 1820. £55

Superb 18th century copper kettle on stand. £65

Large copper kettle, circa 1760. £85

19th century child's chair in elm.   £10

19th century beechwood child's chair with caned seat.   £11

Elm high ladder-back armchair with rush seat.   £30

Windsor stick back armchair, made of ash with elm seat, circa 1810.£45

Elm rocking chair with rush seat, circa 1800.£65

Early elm country armchair on turned legs with stretchers.   £65

A country made rocking chair with bobbin turned splats, circa 1830.   £75

Yew wood Windsor chair with straight legs and crinoline stretcher.   £165

East Anglican oak wainscot chair, circa 1700.   £232

CUPBOARDS

KITCHEN FURNITURE

Victorian stripped pine corner cupboard with glazed doors.   £30

19th century white-painted pine corner cupboard, 2.11 m. high.   £50

A carved oak corner cupboard the panel door with inlaid motifs of shells.£85

George III pinewood corner cupboard.£120

Late 18th century oak corner cupboard with panelled doors.   £160

Queen Anne oak cupboard.   £260

A fine 18th century oak livery cupboard, handles not original, 72in. high.   £300

Massive oak cupboard, 16th century, 49½in. wide, 66in. high. £650

A late 17th century oak tridarn, 53in. wide.   £760

69

Pine dresser with seven
drawers and cupboard,
plate rack above, 5ft.
wide.   **£100**

18th century stripped
pine dresser, 59in.
wide, 17in. deep.**£175**

An early stripped pine
dresser base with rack
added at a later date.
                         £290

An 18th century oak
kitchen dresser,
56½in. wide.   **£380**

An 18th century oak
Welsh dresser with
triple delft rack.**£460**

Georgian oak dresser with
crossbanded drawers and
split baluster moulding,
72in. long.   **£575**

18th century oak
crossbanded
dresser on cabriole
legs.   **£760**

18th century Welsh
oak tridarn.   **£800**

Early 18th century chestnut
dresser, known as a buffet-
vaisselier, 55in. wide. **£945**

SHELVES

KITCHEN FURNITURE

Victorian carved oak open plate rack, 107cm. wide.   £20

Attractive oak Delft rack, circa 1740, 46in. wide x 45½in. high.   £125

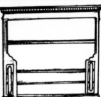

Queen Anne style oak hanging Delft or pewter plate rack, circa 1720.   £225

TABLES

Victorian oak gateleg dining table with a carved border and spiral legs.   £50

17th century oak centre table, 27in. wide.   £80

Farmhouse oak refectory table with honey-coloured patination, circa 1730, 56in. long x 26½in. wide x 29½in. high.   £280

Oak refectory table in original condition, 7ft.1in. long, 29in. wide, circa 1750.   £300

Late 17th century Welsh farmhouse table with an ash top and oak under-frame.   £800

71

KNIFE ACCESSORIES

Victorian country made oak knife box. £10

A brass and steel, desk knife sharpener, with steel roller supports on pillars, circa 1825, 5½in. long, 4in. deep, 3½in. high. £25

Late Victorian knife cleaner. £25

One of a set of four Exeter knife rests, 1861. £45

LADLES

A silver mustard ladle by George Adams, London 1850. £3

Continental silver soup ladle with chased handle 3oz. £6

Continental silver punch ladle, engraved with chased handle. £12

Onslow pattern cream ladle by F. Higgins, 1899. £16

19th century silver ladle. £32

Unmarked Regency punch ladle with turned rosewood handle, 9½in. long. £35

Fiddle pattern cream ladle by J. Bell of Newcastle, 1829. £35

Fluted silver punch ladle by E. Aldridge, 1742. £100

Edwardian metal carrying lamp. £4

Brass travelling lamp with plated reflector. £12

Miller & Co. brass lamp, 9in. high. £12

A brass chamber candle lamp, with globe and crown. £16

19th century tin 'bull's eye' lamp. £18

A ship's brass column globe oil lamp. £20

A brass oil lamp with domed top and glazed front and sides, 12½in. high. £25

A square copper oil lamp, with chimney and glazed sides with bars, 1ft. 3in. high. £30

Queen Anne brass and horn lantern. £80

LAMPS
CYCLE

A Lucas brass gas lamp. £10

A J. Lucas acetyline bicycle lamp, 18cm. high, on a bicycle mounting with a fuel reservoir below. £28

Miller & Co. brass edlite lamp with green and red glass 'bull's eyes' at the sides, the whole on a bicycle mounting, 13cm. high. £50

CARRIAGE

Victorian brass carriage lamp. £25

Old Horse coach lamp in black painted tin, with cut bevelled glass panels, circa 1850. £35

19th century brass carriage lamp. £45

CRUSIE

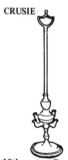

19th century Roman style brass oil lamp. £17

A rare tinned sheet iron double crusie or Betty lamp, with pierced flower discs, circa 1850, 12in. high. £20

An 18th century brass, table crusie lamp, 18½ in. high. £40

A mahogany fluted pillar electric lamp on circular base, with shade. £8

19th century electric lamp, the base with a bronze eagle. £14

A Celadon glazed ware vase-shaped, table electric lamp, on brass base. £30

19th century blue ground earthenware table lamp with a brass top and base, 13½in. tall. £30

Spelter figure lamp, 28½in. high. £35

19th century ornate silver plated electric table lamp, 20in. high. £45

A French ormolu electric table lamp. The stem forming a child in bronze seated on a gilt metal tortoise, 13in. high. £55

A fine Victorian Doulton china lamp, 20in. high. £55

A large ornate brass lamp with crystal glass drops, 24½in. high. £100

LAMPS   FLOOR

19th century
carved oak
floor lamp.
£20

Victorian mahogany
spiral pillar electric
floor lamp on
carved claw feet.
£45

An Indian engraved
brass oil floor lamp
with shade.   £45

A Victorian brass, electric
floor lamp with ball chain
festoons, on a circular
base, with paw feet.   £85

Victorian brass
electric floor
lamp on hoof
feet.   £90

Early 19th century
brass Corinthian
pillar floor lamp,
145cm. high. £120

Unusual plated oil lamp with a Nailsea chimney. £38

A lace maker's glass lamp, 16.5cm. high. £75

A delicate fuschia lamp by Muller Freres, circa 1905. £230

An Art Deco table lamp and shade by Daum, of pink tinted opaque glass having reeded, slightly bulbous stem, 20in. high. £230

A fine late 19th century lamp by Muller. £500

Galle glass table lamp, signed, about 1900, 35cm. high. £530

A superb etched and enamelled glass table lamp. £920

An excellent Tiffany lamp. £4,043

A superb Tiffany Wisteria lamp, 27in. high. £6,500

Victorian brass hanging oil lamp complete with ribbon white shades. £25

Japanese carved wood hexagonal hanging lantern with opaque and decorated glass panels, 61 cm. high. £30

Victorian style hanging oil lamp. £35

A high domed and pierced brass hall lamp, with single suspension handle, 11 in. high, circa 1840. £35

Large Victorian copper street lamp. £40

Brass hall lantern with four leaded stained glass panels, circa 1860, 22 in. high. £45

A fine copper pub lamp, with original green glass, 32 in. high, circa 1850. £100

A 19th century gilt brass hall lantern, of octagonal form, decorated with hooves and ram's heads. £250

George III bronze framed porch lantern. £400

Late 18th century brass
oil lamp. £20

Brass reading lamp
with plated reflector.
£25

A brass table oil lamp.
with a flower painted
globe, 1ft.6in. high.
£28

Brass oil lamp
with pedestal
stem. £28

Victorian brass column
lamp, the clear globe with
embossed design. £30

A tall brass oil lamp
with fluted font and
base, etched globe.
£30

A brass oil lamp with moulded
reservoir, stem and foot and
blue glass shade, 1ft.9in. high.
£30

Victorian brass pedestal
oil lamp fitted with a
frosted and etched globe.
£32

An adjustable, brass,
desk oil lamp with
white shade. £36

A brass Corinthian pillar oil lamp, with glass oil font and shade.   £38

A brass oil lamp with baluster stem, white moulded reservoir and shade.   £38

A brass oil lamp, the reservoir and frosted globe raised on a Corinthian column and moulded base, 2ft.5in. high.   £40

Victorian brass Corinthian column oil lamp with etched cranberry coloured globe.   £44

Victorian brass oil lamp with a green glass shade.   £44

Large Victorian oil lamp with pink column and 9in. etched shade.   £45

A brass circular oil lamp with crimson glass shade, 23in. high.   £46

Victorian brass argand lamp with white glass shades.   £48

A tall brass oil lamp with twin reservoirs and frosted globes.£50

An adjustable oil lamp, with twin burners and green shades. £65

19th century alabaster and brass column table lamp. £65

China vase-shaped oil lamp with brass fittings. £55

Victorian brass oil lamp with a coloured glass shade. £70

A 19th century cut glass oil lamp, on circular base, with shade. £70

Onyx pillar table oil lamp with cloisonne enamel and brass mounts. £75

A very handsome Victorian oil lamp made in bronze and Paris porcelain, circa 1860. £85

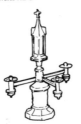

One of a pair of Gothic bronze lamps, 1830, 24in. high. £450

One of a set of four Colza lamps on metal stands. £600

81

LAMPS
WALL

A horsecoach internal spring loaded candle-holder in brass, 6in. high. £28

Victorian brass railway style candle bracket lamp with chimney and coronet. £34

One of a pair of brass wall bracket oil lamps, with green glass shades. £40

One of a pair of brass oil wall lamps, the reservoir supported by dolphins, 1ft.2in. high. £40

One of a pair of Adam,giltwood, wall candle sconces. £110

Small Queen Anne pierced and en-graved wall sconce, about 1714, 6½in. high. £135

LETTER CONTAINERS

19th century brass letter clip by Merry, Phipson & Parker. £6.50

Victorian brass letter rack. £12

Victorian papier mache letter rack. £25

LOG CONTAINERS

A brass bound copper log pail with swing handle. £20

A cylindrical copper log pail, with brass loop handles and paw feet, 10in. high. £25

Victorian copper circular log pail, with brass bands and swing handle. £30

Victorian oak log box with embossed copper lid, 79cm. wide. £34

Circular copper log cauldron with brass handles and claw feet. £35

Wood dyer's iron cauldron used as a log container, circa 1800. £35

A copper oval log cauldron, with brass handles and paw feet. £35

18th century Dutch brass log cauldron on paw feet. £70

Early 19th century pierced brass log box with liner, 13in. high. £80

MEASURES

Tinned iron whisky dipping measure. £5

George III copper measure. £18

A 19th century copper gallon spirit measure. £20

Late 19th century thistle measure with Glasgow tree. £20

Large 19th century lidded Scottish measure. £25

Copper and brass five gallon measure with iron handle. £30

A set of three Victorian copper
measures with iron handles and
brass plate engraved 'Cider'.£35

Bushel corn measure, iron
banded, circa 1840. £37

An interesting one gallon
measure from Woburn Abbey,
10in. high. £40

One gallon copper spirit measure,
dovetail seams, circa 1850. £48

Four gallon copper measure. £55

A copper four gallon measure.
£60

85

Steel banded wooden corn
measure, stamped KP, circa 1790,
16½in. diam, 14in. high.   £60

Brass standard measure, circa
1820.   £75

Set of William IV grain measures in wood.   £75

Set of Irish haystack measures in pewter.   £80

French 19th century pewter,
lidded, double litre measure,
10in.   £90

Early 19th century one gallon
harvest measure with scroll
handle, 11½in. high.   £115

Jersey pewter wine measure of
typical form, about 5½in. high.
                                            £170

Unusual set of three copper and
brass spirit measures, circa 1850,
one gallon, 10½in. high, three
gallons, 16in. high, five gallons,
19in. high.   £194

Standard bronze measure with
container, circa 1601.   £200

Set of ten gun metal standard
capacity measures from bushel
to quarter gill.   £1,000

87

MILKING EQUIPMENT

Small, Victorian brass milk churn. £10

Copper, milkman's cream dipper, 22½in. long, 4in. cup. £12

A milkman's quart tin milk dipper with a curved brass handle to hang on the edge of the churn, circa 1850, 4in. high excluding handle. £14

Pine milk yoke, 36in. long. £15

Victorian copper milk pail with brass handles. £20

18th century steel and copper ladle, 24in. long. £22

Dairy shop's pottery milk bucket, named 'Pure Milk', 12in. high, circa 1850. £68

Copper, milkmaid's bucket with swing over handle, circa 1820. £75

Victorian waffle iron.   £9

Victorian iron cherry seeder.   £15

Late 19th century hour glass egg timer in Mauchline stand.   £8

Georgian brass shoe horn.   £7

19th century beadwork tea cosy.   £9

19th century butcher's bone saw, 23in. long. £34

Late 19th century iron raisin stoner.   £12

Victorian plated egg steamer. £15

Early 20th century English marmalade chopper.   £15

MISCELLANEOUS

One of a pair of
brass bound tubs,
circa 1850.   £95

Edwardian set of
ivory cocktail sticks.
£10

One of a pair of
grocer's display
scuttles decorated
in red and gold,
circa 1820.   £145

American Dover
pattern whisk in
iron with a turned
wood handle,
circa 1904. £2.50

Cast brass bell-shaped butcher's
scale weights, circa 1850, gradu-
ated sizes from 7lb-½oz., nine
in all.   £68

Unusual oblong
shaped wafer
iron for making
wafer bread. £30

Painted metal
stamp.   £3.50

Wooden flour bin
made by a cooper.
£6

Brass 'Man in
the Moon' dish,
circa 1905. £4

MINCING MACHINES

MINCING MACHINES

Late 19th century Enterprise meat chopper.   £5

Cast iron and brass Victorian mincer by Burgess and Key, 13 x 6in.   £38

NIGHTLIGHTS

Victorian green glass night light. £3.50

Staffordshire porcelain pastille burner cottage, circa 1840.   £52

A night light holder bearing various scenes. £80

NUTCRACKERS

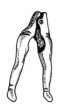

An amusing pair of Victorian brass nutcrackers. £12

An amusing carved wood nutcracker in the form of a grotesque man's head, the jaws cracking the nut, circa 1840.   £18

Victorian silver nut crackers by Edward Edwards, 1841.   £180

NUTMEG GRATERS

Enamel egg-shaped nutmeg grater in yellow and white. £30

Box-type nutmeg grater by William Elliott, 1825.£120

Oval nutmeg grater by Thomas Willmore, 1790. £200

PADLOCKS

Old Spanish padlock and key. £9

Early 19th century French padlock with oak leaf decoration on key escutcheon cover. £10

17th century bar padlock and key. £28

PAILS

Victorian floral toilet pail with a wicker handle. £15

Victorian brass cider pail. £18

One of a set of four Georgian oyster pails in brass bound mahogany, 10in. diameter. £1,500

PASTRY TRIMMERS

Brass pie trimmer and wheel, circa 1830. £5

PASTRY TRIMMERS

Brass pastry jigger and pricker, late 18th century, 4in. long. £11

PESTLE AND MORTARS

Brass pestle and mortar, around 1890. £23

Cast iron pestle and mortar. £24

Early 17th century Dutch bronze pestle and mortar. £340

PLATE WARMERS

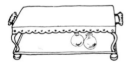

Edwardian double handled copper plate warmer. £16

An oblong copper plate warmer with two burners and brass handles, 2ft.3in. wide. £30

18th century plate warmer. £60

Late 18th century plate warmer in brass and wrought iron, 24in. long. £200

POT LIDS

Uncle Toby . £22

Peace £25

Landing the Fare,
Pegwell Bay. £35

Holy Trinity, Stratford.
£35

Summer. £60

Sea Nymph. £100

Napoleon III with
the Empress
Eugenie. £175

Rare pot lid with
a narrow foliate
border, maker
Robert Feast.
£180

Royal Coat of
Arms. £195

Rare pot lid
with a scene
in Trinidad. £380

Pot lid Pet
Rabbits . £600

Pot lid commemorating
the New York Exhibi-
tion of 1853. £1,000

PRESERVING PANS

PRESERVING PANS

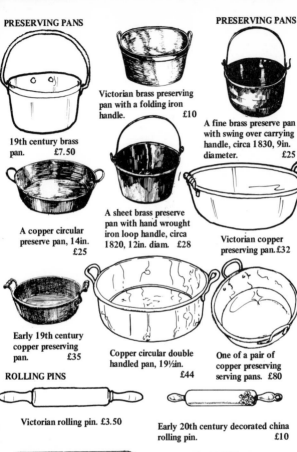

19th century brass pan. £7.50

Victorian brass preserving pan with a folding iron handle. £10

A fine brass preserve pan with swing over carrying handle, circa 1830, 9in. diameter. £25

A copper circular preserve pan, 14in. £25

A sheet brass preserve pan with hand wrought iron loop handle, circa 1820, 12in. diam. £28

Victorian copper preserving pan. £32

Early 19th century copper preserving pan. £35

Copper circular double handled pan, 19½in. £44

One of a pair of copper preserving serving pans. £80

ROLLING PINS

Victorian rolling pin. £3.50

Early 20th century decorated china rolling pin. £10

Victorian glass rolling pin. £20

Bristol blue glass sailor's love token. £28

A wrought iron rush-
light and candleholder
on a wooden base,
17th century.   £48

Early 18th century iron hanging
rushlight and candleholder, 4ft.
long extending to 6ft.   £68

Queen Anne
rushlight holder,
36in. high. £100

A Queen Anne iron
rushlight holder, 48in.
high, circa 1710.£115

Adjustable Queen Anne
wrought iron rushlight
and candle stand, circa
1705.   £125

One of a pair of late
17th century iron
candleholders. £260

SALAD BOWLS SALAD BOWLS

Victorian turned wood salad bowl with servers. £18

Victorian china salad bowl complete with servers. £18

Circular Doulton Lambeth salad bowl having blue and fawn decorations with plated rim and matching plated servers. £60

SALAD SERVERS

Pair of plated salad servers made in 1920's. £4

George III fiddle pattern salad tongs by Ward S. Kingdom, London 1813, 4oz.5dwt. £45

SAMOVARS

19th century copper samovar. £30

Victorian plated on copper samovar complete with burner. £40

Early 19th century copper samovar with lion's head drop ring handles and a brass tap. £55

SAUCEPANS

Four various copper lids. £10

Georgian brass saucepan. £10

Late 19th century copper saucepan with an ebony handle. £12

Victorian copper saucepan complete with lid. £26

George III copper saucepan with wrought steel handle riveted to pan, 9in. diameter. £28

George III copper saucepan complete with lid. £30

An early Victorian copper pan with a wooden handle. £35

Brass skillet by Jeffries and Price, circa 1710. £55

17th century bell metal skillet. £65

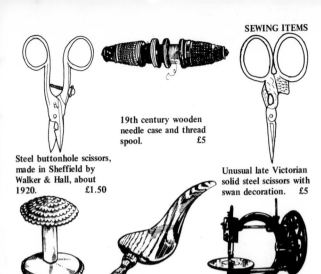

19th century wooden
needle case and thread
spool.   £5

Steel buttonhole scissors,
made in Sheffield by
Walker & Hall, about
1920.   £1.50

Unusual late Victorian
solid steel scissors with
swan decoration.   £5

Victorian ivory
sewing reel. £5

Early wooden knitting sheath
in elm.   £5

Wanzer lock stitch
sewing machine on
marble base.   £15

Brass 'Humming Bird'
surmounted with a
pincushion.   £30

Regency period ormolu
reel stand with the orig-
inal reels.   £35

19th century treen
two-tier reel stand
on three bun feet
in mahogany. £42

99

SCALES

Polished steelyard sack scales, complete with pear shaped weight, circa 1790, 25in. long. £22

Victorian brass letter scales. £26

Victorian kitchen scales with brass pans and cast iron stand. £30

Late Victorian, grocer's scales. £32

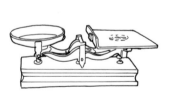

A large pair of 19th century cast iron scales. £40

Pair of grocer's weighing scales on mahogany base, with brass fittings and weights, by W. & T. Avery. £50

SCOOPS

Silver cream scoop with rat-tail and wood handle. £15

Marrow scoop by Samuel Godbehere. £45

SCOOPS

Marrow scoop, Samuel Pemberton, Birmingham, 1802. £32

Combined silver marrow scoop and table spoon by Elias Cachart, 1750. £85

SIGNS

Tin advertisement for Pearson's Antiseptic. £10

A rare English enamelled advertising sign designed by the 'Beggarstaffs', 21 x 14in, circa 1905. £15

Bovril poster mounted on stretched canvas, 5ft. x 3ft.4in., circa 1940. £40

A Crosse & Blackwell advertising plaque stamped 'TJ and J. Mayer', 24cm. x 32cm. £440

SIEVES

Victorian wooden sieve. £2.50

19th century brass sieve. £16

An unusual 19th century sieve enclosed in copper oval container, complete with carrying handles, circa 1850. £48

SKEWERS

Silver skewer, 1902. £20

Silver meat skewer by Wallace and Hayne, London 1819. £55

Meat skewer by Wallace and Hayne, London, 1819. £60

Pair of silver meat skewers by Peter and Ann Bateman, 1798. £60

SKIMMERS

Brass skimmer with pierced handle. £8

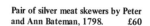

Salamander, a hot metal plate for browning food. £12

Cook's copper cream skimmer with wrought iron handle, circa 1790. £19

18th century brass skimmer. £27

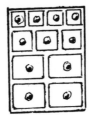

Japanned spice box, black with gilt decoration. £7

Pinewood spice drawers with brass pulls, circa 1820, 14½in. high x 11½in. x 7in. £56

Small oak spice cupboard with eight interior drawers, circa 1690. £125

SPITS

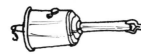

19th century brass roasting jack. £16

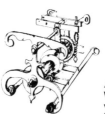

A rare polished steel larkspit, 30½in. high, circa 1750. £45

Rare steel spitjack, circa 1700. £245

A superb example of a William and Mary period wrought iron meat spit-jack, with original cast iron driving weight and wheel governor, 12in. high, circa 1690. £275

SPOONS

Large Victorian wooden spoon. £5

Early Scottish horn spoon.   £7

Victorian silver berry spoon. £24

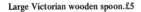

Early Georgian cast silver mote spoon.   £35

STICKSTANDS

Victorian embossed brass oval stickstand.
£16

An embossed brass and oak half circle stickstand, 2ft.7in. high.   £25

Cast iron Gothic revival umbrella stand, about 1860, 30in. high.   £275

STOCKPOTS

Victorian polished steel cooking pot.   £10

Large copper stockpot with lid, circa 1820, 12in. diameter.   £50

A polished copper stockpot, complete with brass tap and copper carrying handles, circa 1820, 13in. diameter.   £75

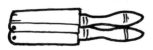

Wooden lemon squeezer with rounded place for half lemon. £3

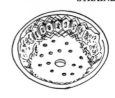

Victorian china water cress dish. £6

Early 20th century china tea strainer.   £6

George I silver lemon strainer by Francis Knelme, London 1727.   £125

Silver lemon strainer by H. Northcote, 1799.   £150

Unusual bright-cut silver strainer, 1778, 10in. across.   £150

Large silver punch strainer by Robert Calderwood, Dublin, 1752, 11½in. long, 6oz. 5dwt.   £375

Early 18th century silver lemon strainer by Thomas Bamford, 6in. long, 2oz. 4dwt.   £450

105

STRING HOLDERS

Victorian papier mache string holder.   £8

A late 19th century transfer-printed souvenir box.   £10

Yew wood string holder with ridged decoration.   £11

SUGAR CUTTERS

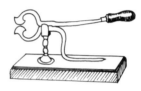

Steel sugar cutters, circa 1790. £12

Pair of 18th century brass sugar cutters on a mahogany stand.£25

TAPER LAMPS

A rare 19th century cast iron wick lamp with detachable screw off lid and swing carrying handle, 11in. high.   £35

Late 18th century brass taper jack, 5½in. high.   £82

Taperstick by Christian Hammer in the form of a sandalled foot, Stockholm, 1857, 5¼in. long.   £100

Victorian red enamel teapot.   £3

Edwardian silver lustre teapot and
stand.   £4.50

19th century Japanese copper
teapot with gilt decoration. £7

Staffordshire teapot of William IV
silver design.   £7.50

Liverpool teapot enamelled in black
and gilding, Herculaneum factory,
circa 1805.   £20

Flamboyant green, yellow, gold and
white teapot, made by Samuel
Alcock, 1843.   £28

Newhall teapot, pattern 436, circa
1795.   £55

William Moorcroft teapot 1898,
painted with blue poppies.   £60

TEAPOTS

Boat shaped teapot, about 1810, possibly from the Sewell pottery. £67

Derby teapot decorated with a traditional Imari pattern. £75

Worcester teapot, marked Barr, Flight and Barr, 1807-1813. £110

18th century saltglaze teapot with painted and relief decoration, 3½in. high. £155

Liverpool teapot and cover with artichoke finial, 4¼in. high, circa 1770. £180

Worcester teapot and cover depicting 'The Beckoning Chinaman', circa 1755, 6¼in. high. £220

Saltglaze ermine spot teapot. £600

Rare slatglaze, blue ground, teapot and cover of globular form, circa 1760, 3¼in. high. £820

Miniature tin of
Andrews Liver Salts
produced by LNER
trains, circa 1930. £3

Caleys Jazz-Time toffee
tin, circa 1920.   £5

Mackintosh's toffee
shop, circa 1930. £6

A large confectionery
tin by John Buchanan,
Glasgow, 8¾in. wide,
circa 1890.   £6

Rowntrees toffee
tin, circa 1930. £8

W & R Jacob biscuit
tin in the form of a
Jacobean log box. £8

Victorian black
japanned tea
canister, decor-
ated with Chinese
gilt design, 17in.
high.   £8

Huntley and Palmer tin,
decorated with printed
paper, circa 1900.   £10

Decorated mustard tin
showing National
Games.   £14

TOAST RACKS

19th century plated toast rack. £9

Toast rack by Walker and Hall, 1899, 7oz. £32

Victorian toast rack by Robert Garrard, London 1869. £85

TOASTING FORKS

An early sycamore and walnut, steel toasting fork. £25

17th century brass and iron trivet toaster, 25in. long. £30

Silver toasting fork by Joseph Willmore, 1806. £70

George III Scottish bannock toaster, 27½in. long overall, Edinburgh 1819. £220

TOWEL RAILS

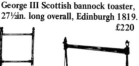

Victorian mahogany triple towel rail. £16

A late 18th century mahogany towel airer of two folding leaves, with boxwood stringing. £22

Hepplewhite design towel horse, 2ft. £40

Large Indian brass tray, 2ft. wide. £12

A Victorian oak tray with carved vine border and brass handles, 2ft. wide. £12

Edwardian oak double handled octagonal tea tray. £16

Mahogany inlaid oval tea tray with brass handles, 26½in. £16

Oriental copper circular tray with wavy border. £16

19th century walnut butler's tray. £18

Late 19th century butler's oak tray and folding stand. £18

Benares damascened circular coffee tray on a folding stand, 23in. diam. £18

George III mahogany tray inlaid
with a conch shell.   £20

Large copper circular tray with
fluted border.   £20

An Indian brass oblong double
handled tea tray, 19in. wide. £22

Edwardian mahogany kidney-
shaped tray with marquetry
centre, 23in. wide.   £25

A walnut and parquetry inlaid
oblong tray with chess board and
brass handles, 20½in. wide.   £26

An Oriental brass circular shaped
coffee tray, 56cm. diameter, on
carved wood stand.   £26

A mahogany sectioned oval tea
tray with pierced brass gallery,
33in. wide.   £28

A 19th century Toleware tea
tray with floral pattern in the
centre, 26½in. x 20½in.   £30

Regency mahogany and brass handled oval tea tray inlaid with orchids and ribbons in boxwood, holly and harewoods.   £40

Victorian papier mache oval tray painted with flowers enhanced by mother-of-pearl, 75cm. wide.
£40

Butchers' boy's shoulder meat carrier, circa 1810.   £48

A japanned tray, decorated with a vase of flowers, 2ft.8in.
£50

English Regency 'Pontypool' tray, black with gilt decoration, approximately 25 x 18in., circa 1810.   £65

A 19th century japanned oval tray with gilt mother-of-pearl flower decoration, 31in. wide.
£65

A 19th century papier mache oblong tray painted with a Chinese landscape in gilt, 2ft.6in.   £85

Victorian papier mache tray, 25in.   £90

George III papier mache tray by Henry Clay, 27in. wide, with matching teapot stand. £96

A 19th century butler's mahogany oblong tray with folding sides, on folding stand. £100

'Pontypool' tray with Napoleonic battle scene, circa 1820, 30in. x 21in. £105

A metal tray with pierced gallery decorated with an urn, flowers and birds, 2ft.3in. wide. £110

19th century papier mache tray by Clay. £125

English black and gold papier mache tray, signed Jennens and Bettridge, approximately 30 x 22in., circa 1830. £130

Georgian mahogany butler's tray complete with stand. £165

A square Japanese lacquer chamfered tray, 16½in. wide. £560

114

19th century Irish, iron horse shoe trivet. £10

Victorian brass trivet with a turned wood handle. £10

Victorian brass trivet with screw on legs. £10

Victorian brass trivet. £12

Late 18th century brass trivet with ebony handle. £18

Georgian brass trivet. £24

A heavy polished steel Queen Anne trivet, circa 1710, 13in. high, 10in. diameter. £30

Wrought iron trivet, circa 1740. £38

Fireside trivet in wrought iron with heavy pierced brass top and turned fruitwood handle, circa 1750. £38

115

TUREENS

Doulton tureen with
floral decoration,
circa 1900.   £12

Royal Worcester tureen
decorated in gold, circa
1889.   £15

"Gothic Castle"
vegetable tureen,
marked Spode.
£25

Minton tureen with
domed cover, circa
1868.   £30

Blue printed Spode
tureen, circa 1830.
£45

Masons ironstone
tureen, circa 1830.
£65

Minton game tureen,
circa 1873.   £65

Early 19th century
Meissen tureen,
43cm. wide.   £85

Worcester blue and
white tureen and
cover, circa 1758.
£260

Victorian copper urn with brass top.   £18

A copper circular vase shaped tea urn with brass handles and spout, 13½in. high.   £32

A George III brass globular tea urn, on four legs and ball feet.   £45

Doulton Lambeth urn with raised stag and foliage decoration, 16in. high.   £55

Decorative large copper and brass George III tea urn, 22in. high.   £58

Early 19th century copper urn.   £70

A gigantic toleware, copper and brass tea urn, originally used as a grocer's shop sign, circa 1850. £80

An 18th century copper urn with brass tap.   £85

A fine Sheffield vase shaped tea urn with scrolled handles and chased and gadrooned borders.   £150

VACUUM CLEANERS

Hand operated B.V.C. vacuum
cleaner, circa 1910.   £60

An early English vacuum cleaner,
with iron-spoked wheels and
rubber tyres, 3ft.10in. high, circa
1900.   £100

VEGETABLE CHOPPERS

Mincing knife or
suet chopper for
use on a board.
              £4

Mincing knife or
suet chopper for
use on a board
and with a bowl.
              £4

19th century
wooden cabbage
slicer.   £15

Large, Victorian kraut cutter of
wood and brass.   £20

Swedish steel vegetable chopper.
                        £24

A 19th century brass bed warming pan, with long wood handle .£35

19th century copper warming pan.   £40

George III copper bed warming pan, circa 1760, 39in. long.   £52

George II copper warming pan engraved with floral design.£60

18th century copper warming pan with a turned fruitwood handle.   £60

17th century brass warming pan with iron handle.   £65

119

WASH BOILERS

Solid copper wash boiler, with turned over rim, circa 1830, 17in. diam., 13in. high. £30

Late 19th century copper wash boiler. £35

A large, solid copper wash boiler, the side seam and band near base with large copper rivets, circa 1820, 14in. high, 20in. diam. £35

WASHING EQUIPMENT

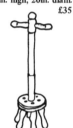

Late 19th century glass and wood scrubbing board. £3

A wooden sock stretcher, one of a pair. £5

Pine and elm dolly for washing clothes. £7.50

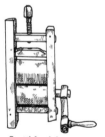

Scottish miniature wooden mangle for clerical bands. £15

Late 19th century mangle. £25

Late 19th century wood and iron rotary washer. £30

120

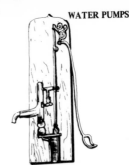

Polished steel, bronze and brass water pump, in working order, circa 1800. £85

Highly polished brass, steel and lead farmhouse kitchen water pump. £85

WATERING CANS

19th century English brass watering can. £8

A Victorian brass water can, 11in. high. £12

19th century brass watering can. £12

Victorian copper watering can. £15

A copper gallon water can with a swing handle and a brass loop handle. £18

An oval lidded copper watering can, the body with moulded banding. £20

WINE COOLERS

Mid 19th century Bristol clear glass wine cooler with characteristic prismatic cutting round the neck. £40

A gilded blue glass tulip design wine cooler signed by Isaac and Lazarus. £250

Porcelain ice-bucket from the Nymphenburg factory, 6½in. high. £500

WINE FUNNELS

Sheffield plate wine funnel, about 1810, with unusual ribbed strengthening section on spout. £40

A silver wine funnel by George Lowe, Newcastle, 1824. £105

Mid 18th century Worcester poly-chromed wine funnel, 5½in. tall. £4,400

YEAST VESSELS

Copper brewer's yeast vessel with loop handle and long pouring spout, circa 1890, 10in. high. £56

An 18th century copper, brewer's yeast vessel. £75

INDEX

124